HAL•LEONARD
INSTRUMENTAL
PLAY-ALONG

🔊 AUDIO
ACCESS
INCLUDED

PLAYBACK+
Speed • Pitch • Balance • Loop

CLARINET
JAZZ BLUES
FAVORITES

T0070462

Audio arrangements by Peter Deneff

To access audio visit:
www.halleonard.com/mylibrary

Enter Code
3343-9215-0202-2122

ISBN 978-1-4950-5336-8

7777 W. BLUEMOUND RD. P.O. BOX 13819 MILWAUKEE, WI 53213

Visit Hal Leonard Online at
www.halleonard.com

ALL BLUES

Clarinet

By MILES DAVIS

BASIN STREET BLUES

Clarinet

Words and Music by
SPENCER WILLIAMS

BIRK'S WORKS

Clarinet

By DIZZY GILLESPIE

C-JAM BLUES

Clarinet

By DUKE ELLINGTON

FREDDIE FREELOADER

Clarinet

By MILES DAVIS

MR. P.C.

CLARINET

By JOHN COLTRANE

NIGHT TRAIN

Clarinet

Words by OSCAR WASHINGTON
and LEWIS C. SIMPKINS
Music by JIMMY FORREST

NOW'S THE TIME

Clarinet

By CHARLIE PARKER

ONE FOR DADDY-O

Clarinet

By NAT ADDERLY

THE SWINGIN' SHEPHERD BLUES

Clarinet

Words and Music by MOE KOFFMAN,
RHODA ROBERTS and KENNY JACOBSON

TENOR MADNESS

Clarinet

By SONNY ROLLINS

THINGS AIN'T WHAT THEY USED TO BE

Clarinet

By MERCER ELLINGTON

Chart Hits

All About That Bass • All of Me • Happy • Radioactive • Roar • Say Something • Shake It Off • A Sky Full of Stars • Someone like You • Stay with Me • Thinking Out Loud • Uptown Funk.

_____00146207	Flute	$12.99
_____00146208	Clarinet	$12.99
_____00146209	Alto Sax	$12.99
_____00146210	Tenor Sax	$12.99
_____00146211	Trumpet	$12.99
_____00146212	Horn	$12.99
_____00146213	Trombone	$12.99
_____00146214	Violin	$12.99
_____00146215	Viola	$12.99
_____00146216	Cello	$12.99

Coldplay

Clocks • Every Teardrop Is a Waterfall • Fix You • In My Place • Lost! • Paradise • The Scientist • Speed of Sound • Trouble • Violet Hill • Viva La Vida • Yellow.

_____00103337	Flute	$12.99
_____00103338	Clarinet	$12.99
_____00103339	Alto Sax	$12.99
_____00103340	Tenor Sax	$12.99
_____00103341	Trumpet	$12.99
_____00103342	Horn	$12.99
_____00103343	Trombone	$12.99
_____00103344	Violin	$12.99
_____00103345	Viola	$12.99
_____00103346	Cello	$12.99

Disney Greats

Arabian Nights • Hawaiian Roller Coaster Ride • It's a Small World • Look Through My Eyes • Yo Ho (A Pirate's Life for Me) • and more.

_____00841934	Flute	$12.99
_____00841935	Clarinet	$12.99
_____00841936	Alto Sax	$12.99
_____00841937	Tenor Sax	$12.95
_____00841938	Trumpet	$12.99
_____00841939	Horn	$12.95
_____00841940	Trombone	$12.95
_____00841941	Violin	$12.99
_____00841942	Viola	$12.95
_____00841943	Cello	$12.99
_____00842078	Oboe	$12.99

Great Themes

Bella's Lullaby • Chariots of Fire • Get Smart • Hawaii Five-O Theme • I Love Lucy • The Odd Couple • Spanish Flea • and more.

_____00842468	Flute	$12.99
_____00842469	Clarinet	$12.99
_____00842470	Alto Sax	$12.99
_____00842471	Tenor Sax	$12.99
_____00842472	Trumpet	$12.99
_____00842473	Horn	$12.99
_____00842474	Trombone	$12.99
_____00842475	Violin	$12.99
_____00842476	Viola	$12.99
_____00842477	Cello	$12.99

Lennon & McCartney Favorites

All You Need Is Love • A Hard Day's Night • Here, There and Everywhere • Hey Jude • Let It Be • Nowhere Man • Penny Lane • She Loves You • When I'm Sixty-Four • and more.

_____00842600	Flute	$12.99
_____00842601	Clarinet	$12.99
_____00842603	Tenor Sax	$12.99
_____00842604	Trumpet	$12.99
_____00842605	Horn	$12.99
_____00842607	Violin	$12.99
_____00842608	Viola	$12.99
_____00842609	Cello	$12.99

Popular Hits

Breakeven • Fireflies • Halo • Hey, Soul Sister • I Gotta Feeling • I'm Yours • Need You Now • Poker Face • Viva La Vida • You Belong with Me • and more.

_____00842511	Flute	$12.99
_____00842512	Clarinet	$12.99
_____00842513	Alto Sax	$12.99
_____00842514	Tenor Sax	$12.99
_____00842515	Trumpet	$12.99
_____00842516	Horn	$12.99
_____00842517	Trombone	$12.99
_____00842518	Violin	$12.99
_____00842519	Viola	$12.99
_____00842520	Cello	$12.99

Songs from Frozen, Tangled and Enchanted

Do You Want to Build a Snowman? • For the First Time in Forever • Happy Working Song • I See the Light • In Summer • Let It Go • Mother Knows Best • That's How You Know • True Love's First Kiss • When Will My Life Begin • and more.

_____00126921	Flute	$14.99
_____00126922	Clarinet	$14.99
_____00126923	Alto Sax	$14.99
_____00126924	Tenor Sax	$14.99
_____00126925	Trumpet	$14.99
_____00126926	Horn	$14.99
_____00126927	Trombone	$14.99
_____00126928	Violin	$14.99
_____00126929	Viola	$14.99
_____00126930	Cello	$14.99

Top Hits

Adventure of a Lifetime • Budapest • Die a Happy Man • Ex's & Oh's • Fight Song • Hello • Let It Go • Love Yourself • One Call Away • Pillowtalk • Stitches • Writing's on the Wall.

_____00171073	Flute	$12.99
_____00171074	Clarinet	$12.99
_____00171075	Alto Sax	$12.99
_____00171106	Tenor Sax	$12.99
_____00171107	Trumpet	$12.99
_____00171108	Horn	$12.99
_____00171109	Trombone	$12.99
_____00171110	Violin	$12.99
_____00171111	Viola	$12.99
_____00171112	Cello	$12.99

Wicked

As Long As You're Mine • Dancing Through Life • Defying Gravity • For Good • I'm Not That Girl • Popular • The Wizard and I • and more.

_____00842236	Flute	$12.99
_____00842237	Clarinet	$11.99
_____00842238	Alto Saxophone	$11.95
_____00842239	Tenor Saxophone	$11.95
_____00842240	Trumpet	$11.99
_____00842241	Horn	$11.95
_____00842242	Trombone	$12.99
_____00842243	Violin	$11.99
_____00842244	Viola	$12.99
_____00842245	Cello	$12.99

HAL•LEONARD®

101 SONGS

YOUR FAVORITE SONGS ARE ARRANGED FOR SOLO INSTRUMENTALISTS WITH THIS GREAT SERIES.

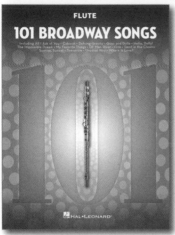

FLUTE
101 BROADWAY SONGS

101 BROADWAY SONGS

Cabaret • Do You Hear the People Sing? • Edelweiss • Guys and Dolls • Hello, Dolly! • I Dreamed a Dream • If I Were a Bell • Luck Be a Lady • Ol' Man River • Seasons of Love • Send in the Clowns • Think of Me • Tomorrow • What I Did for Love • and many more.

00154199	Flute	$14.99
00154200	Clarinet	$14.99
00154201	Alto Sax	$14.99
00154202	Tenor Sax	$14.99
00154203	Trumpet	$14.99
00154204	Horn	$14.99
00154205	Trombone	$14.99
00154206	Violin	$14.99
00154207	Viola	$14.99
00154208	Cello	$14.99

CELLO
101 HIT SONGS

101 HIT SONGS

All About That Bass • All of Me • Brave • Breakaway • Clocks • Fields of Gold • Firework • Hey, Soul Sister • Ho Hey • I Gotta Feeling • Jar of Hearts • Love Story • 100 Years • Roar • Rolling in the Deep • Shake It Off • Smells like Teen Spirit • Uptown Funk • and more.

00194561	Flute	$16.99
00197182	Clarinet	$16.99
00197183	Alto Sax	$16.99
00197184	Tenor Sax	$16.99
00197185	Trumpet	$16.99
00197186	Horn	$16.99
00197187	Trombone	$16.99
00197188	Violin	$16.99
00197189	Viola	$16.99
00197190	Cello	$16.99

VIOLIN
101 CLASSICAL THEMES

101 CLASSICAL THEMES

Ave Maria • Bist du bei mir (You Are with Me) • Canon in D • Clair de Lune • Dance of the Sugar Plum Fairy • 1812 Overture • Eine Kleine Nachtmusik ("Serenade"), First Movement Excerpt • The Flight of the Bumble Bee • Funeral March of a Marionette • Fur Elise • Gymnopedie No. 1 • Jesu, Joy of Man's Desiring • Lullaby • Minuet in G • Ode to Joy • Piano Sonata in C • Pie Jesu • Rondeau • Theme from Swan Lake • Wedding March • William Tell Overture • and many more.

00155315	Flute	$14.99
00155317	Clarinet	$14.99
00155318	Alto Sax	$14.99
00155319	Tenor Sax	$14.99
00155320	Trumpet	$14.99
00155321	Horn	$14.99
00155322	Trombone	$14.99
00155323	Violin	$14.99
00155324	Viola	$14.99
00155325	Cello	$14.99

TRUMPET
101 JAZZ SONGS

101 JAZZ SONGS

All of Me • Autumn Leaves • Bewitched • Blue Skies • Body and Soul • Cheek to Cheek • Come Rain or Come Shine • Don't Get Around Much Anymore • A Fine Romance • Here's to Life • I Could Write a Book • It Could Happen to You • The Lady Is a Tramp • Like Someone in Love • Lullaby of Birdland • The Nearness of You • On Green Dolphin Street • Satin Doll • Stella by Starlight • Tangerine • Unforgettable • The Way You Look Tonight • Yesterdays • and many more.

00146363	Flute	$14.99
00146364	Clarinet	$14.99
00146366	Alto Sax	$14.99
00146367	Tenor Sax	$14.99
00146368	Trumpet	$14.99
00146369	Horn	$14.99
00146370	Trombone	$14.99
00146371	Violin	$14.99
00146372	Viola	$14.99
00146373	Cello	$14.99

HAL•LEONARD®

www.halleonard.com

Prices, contents and availability subject to change without notice.

O217